DATE DUE

Chapter 1

CREATURE FEATURE

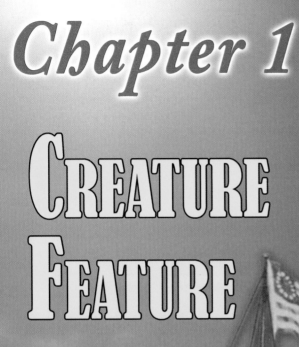

- *September 22:* The Nez Perce send guides with the Corps to the Columbia River.

- *October 16:* The Corps reaches the Columbia River.

- *November 7:* Clark writes his most famous journal entry, "Ocian in view! O! the joy."

- *December 8:* The Corps builds Fort Clatsop on the Columbia River.

1806—*March 22–23:* The Corps of Discovery heads home.

- *July 3:* The Corps crosses the Bitterroot Mountains and breaks into smaller parties to explore the Yellowstone and Marias rivers.

- *July 26–27:* Lewis's party encounters eight Blackfeet warriors. Captain Lewis and Reuben Field kill two when the Blackfeet attempt to steal their horses and guns.

- *August 12–14:* The parties reunite below the Yellowstone River and return to the Mandan villages. Sacagawea remains with the Hidatsa.

- *September 23:* The Corps of Discovery arrives in St. Louis.

- *Fall:* Captains Lewis and Clark finally return to Washington, D.C.

1809—*October 11:* Meriwether Lewis commits suicide at Grinders Stand, an inn south of Nashville, Tennessee.

1812—*December 20:* Sacagawea dies at Fort Manuel.

1838—*September 1:* William Clark dies at the home of his eldest son, Meriwether Lewis Clark.

Explorer Timeline

1770—*August 1:* William Clark is born in Caroline County, Virginia.

1774—*August 18:* Meriwether Lewis is born in Albemarle County, Virginia.

1803—*Spring:* President Thomas Jefferson appoints Meriwether Lewis as military commander of a western expedition. Lewis asks his friend William Clark to join him.

—*July 4:* The Louisiana Purchase doubles the size of the United States.

—*October 26:* Captains Lewis and Clark set out from the Falls of the Ohio.

1804—*May 14:* The Corps of Discovery heads up the Missouri River.

—*August 3:* The Corps holds the first official council between U.S. representatives and American Indians.

—*August 20:* Sergeant Charles Floyd dies near present-day Sioux City, Iowa.

—*November 4:* The Corps hires a French-Canadian, Toussaint Charbonneau, as their interpreter. Sacagawea, his wife, joins the expedition.

1805—*February 11:* Sacagawea gives birth to a son.

—*June 13:* The Corps reaches the Great Falls of the Missouri and discovers five falls.

—*August 17:* Lewis finds the Shoshone. Sacagawea recognizes Shoshone chief Cameahwait as her brother. Lewis and Clark name this site Camp Fortunate.

Contents

Library of Congress Cataloging-in-Publication Data

Robinson, Kate, 1953-
 Lewis and Clark : exploring the American West / Kate Robinson.
   p. cm. — (Great explorers of the world)
 Includes bibliographical references and index.
 Summary: "Examines the Lewis and Clark expedition, including both explorers' early lives, their journey to the Pacific, its impact on the United States and American Indians, and their legacy in American history"—Provided by publisher.
 ISBN-13: 978-1-59845-124-5
 ISBN-10: 1-59845-124-3
 1. Lewis and Clark Expedition (1804-1806)—Juvenile literature. 2. West (U.S.)—Discovery and exploration—Juvenile literature. 3. West (U.S.)—Description and travel—Juvenile literature. 4. Lewis, Meriwether, 1774-1809—Juvenile literature. 5. Clark, William, 1770-1838—Juvenile literature. 6. Explorers—West (U.S.)—Biography—Juvenile literature. I. Title.
 F592.7.R624 2009
 917.804'2—dc22
                2008054037

Printed in the United States of America

112009 Lake Book Manufacturing, Inc., Melrose Park, IL

10 9 8 7 6 5 4 3 2 1

To Our Readers:
We have done our best to make sure all Internet Addresses in this book were active and appropriate when we went to press. However, the author and the publisher have no control over and assume no liability for the material available on those Internet sites or on other Web sites they may link to. Any comments or suggestions can be sent by e-mail to comments@enslow.com or to the address on the back cover.

♻ Enslow Publishers, Inc., is committed to printing our books on recycled paper. The paper in every book contains 10% to 30% post-consumer waste (PCW). The cover board on the outside of each book contains 100% PCW. Our goal is to do our part to help young people and the environment too!

Illustration Credits: American Philosophical Society, pp. 74, 77; Associated Press, p. 88; Clipart.com, p. 48; Donna Neary / National Guard, p. 19; Enslow Publishers, Inc., p. 36; The Granger Collection, New York, pp. 39, 70, 78, 87; Courtesy of Independence National Historical Park, p. 1; © Jupiterimages Corporation, p. 24; Keith Rocco, courtesy of the National Park Service, pp. 27, 43; Library of Congress, pp. 9, 10, 99; © Marilyn Angel / Nativestock.com, p. 92; © North Wind Picture Archives, p. 68; © Shutterstock ®, pp. 61, 80, 101.

Ship Illustration Used in Chapter Openers: Clipart.com.

Cover Illustration: Courtesy of Independence National Historical Park (Portraits of Meriwether Lewis and William Clark).

LEWIS AND CLARK

Great Explorers of the World

Exploring the American West

Kate Robinson

Lewis

Clark

Enslow Publishers, Inc.
40 Industrial Road
Box 398
Berkeley Heights, NJ 07922
USA
http://www.enslow.com

The unmapped upper Missouri River was a mystery to the Corps of Discovery. But the Hidatsa Indians who lived along it knew the river well. They advised Captains Lewis and Clark at Fort Mandan during the long freezing winter of 1804–1805. They said the Corps would have to portage—carry—their boats and equipment around a great waterfall. It might take half a day. Then the Missouri would take the expedition into the Columbia River drainage.[1]

On June 14, 1805, Captain Meriwether Lewis began to scout alone through the low slopes along the Medicine River. His small party had just explored the Great Falls of the Missouri River. Lewis had to make sure he carried out President Thomas Jefferson's orders to find the best water route to the Pacific.

Captain Lewis could see that the portage around the Great Falls would take much longer than half a day. Disappointed and worried, his thoughts drifted as he observed an immense herd of buffalo grazing near the river. It was the largest herd he had seen so far, perhaps the largest herd ever seen by a white man.

Captain Lewis climbed down the hill. He chose a buffalo, raised his rifle and shot it through the lungs. He stared at the blood pouring from the buffalo's mouth and nostrils. Surprised it did not immediately fall, he forgot to reload his rifle. Suddenly, he noticed a large "white" (a grizzly) bear only twenty strides away.[2]

Lewis raised his rifle again. There was no time to reload his weapon. The grizzly bore down on him. Desperate for a place to hide, he glanced around the level plain: no bushes for miles around and the nearest tree stood three hundred yards away. The riverbank, sloped only three feet above the water, was his only hope.

Lewis wanted to make the bear swim. He turned and ran into the river. The grizzly dashed at him full speed, his open jaw bristling with huge teeth. Water sprayed around Lewis like bright crystals in the sunlight as he slogged eighty yards into the center of the river.

Maybe he could not escape the bear in waist-deep water. Lewis spun around and pointed his espontoon, a spear, at the ferocious creature. When the bear came within twenty feet it stared hard at him and suddenly wheeled about. Lewis watched the bear while it ran away. The bear often looked back as if it expected Lewis to follow.

This 1810 woodcut, based on Corps member Patrick Gass's journal, shows a grizzly bear chasing a Corps member into a tree. Lewis had a difficult time evading a grizzly at the Medicine River.

Breathing a long sigh of relief, Lewis straggled through the water to the riverbank. He studied the claw marks in the earth while he reloaded his rifle. He vowed never to delay reloading again. Then he heard a noise. Another four-legged creature, one he had never seen before, crept through the underbrush. Was it a wolf or a cougar? When

Lewis and many other members of his expedition hunted along the riverbanks they explored.

Lewis was within sixty yards of the animal, the tracks looked like some sort of "tiger cat," but he did not know what to call it. Modern historians and scientists think it was a wolverine.[3]

Using his espontoon to steady his rifle, Lewis aimed and fired. The animal disappeared into its burrow. Lewis scolded himself again. First, he had forgotten to load the weapon his life depended upon. Then he had missed an easy shot.

After walking another three hundred yards, Lewis spotted three bull buffalo that had separated from the herd grazing a half-mile away. They started running full-speed at him. Amused, he ran head-on toward the buffalo. At least he would have some fun this time. Just one hundred yards away, the buffalo stopped. Then they turned and retreated as fast as they had approached. Were the bear, the bulls, and the other unknown animals simply curious about him?

Lewis turned around and returned to the buffalo carcass. He decided to go all the way back to base camp at the foot of the first falls. "It now seemed to me that all the beasts of the neighbourhood had made a league to destroy me," he wrote. "I did not think it prudent to remain all night at this place which . . . wore the impression on my mind of inchantment."[4]

The next morning Captain Lewis wrote twenty-four hundred words about his strange experiences with the bear, wolverine, and buffalo. Later, he napped. When he awoke, the "creature feature" continued. A large rattlesnake was coiled on the downed trunk of a tree only ten feet away. It rattled, ready to strike. Lewis killed it—how, he did not say. But he reported details about the snake's anatomy in his journal.[5]

Lewis, Clark, and the Corps of Discovery found many "creatures" and plant species. They also interacted with several American Indian nations during their journey west.

Few events in American history are as alive today as the epic journey of Lewis and Clark.

Chapter 2

WESTWARD VIEW

TWO explorers, Meriwether Lewis and William Clark, were born in Virginia on the eve of the American Revolution. Their families were landholders. In the late eighteenth century, authorities granted large tracts of land to important people. These landholders created large farms, often with slave labor, called plantations. Plantation life was just a generation old, and wild game roamed the woods. Still, people wanted to explore and settle new land outside of the colonies.

American colonists, and, later, the American government, were curious about the frontier beyond the Allegheny Mountains. They wanted more land for the new nation. But it seemed impossible for the United States to control the entire continent. Distances between settlements in the new states were far too great. People traveled by foot, by horse or mule, or in hand-paddled boats and sailing ships. Mountain ranges and river crossings slowed down trade and settlement. It was easier for people on the Atlantic Coast to trade with Great Britain than to trade with Ohio and Kentucky. Natural barriers stopped westward settlement more than international borders or violent American Indian opposition.

THE LEWIS FAMILY

Meriwether Lewis was born on August 18, 1774, in Albemarle County, Virginia. The room he was born in looked out over the Blue Ridge Mountains. The westward view seemed to invite "discovery" of the frontier.

Thomas Jefferson called the Lewis family "one of the most distinguished families" of Virginia.[1] Meriwether's great-grandfather was a Welsh officer in the British Army. Robert Lewis arrived in Virginia in 1635 with a land grant from the British king of 33,333 acres. He willed the land to his son, Colonel Robert Lewis. Colonel Lewis willed substantial lands and homes to each of his nine children. The colonel's son William inherited slaves, as well as 1,896 acres and a rustic log house called Locust Hill. This estate sat near the hilltop where Thomas Jefferson built his plantation estate, Monticello.

William Lewis married his cousin Lucy in 1769. Lucy Meriwether's family was also land-rich. The Revolutionary War broke out in 1775 when their son Meriwether was just a baby. William Lewis volunteered to serve with one of the first military regiments raised in the

Virginia area. In November 1779, after a short leave visiting his family, William Lewis attempted to cross at Secretary's Ford on the Rivanna River. He fell from his horse into the icy water. He died of pneumonia.

Five-year-old Meriwether barely knew his father. Lucy Meriwether remarried in the spring of 1780. Her second husband, John Marks, took the family south to the Broad River Valley in northern Georgia. They joined other Virginians who moved to the frontier colony developed by General John Matthews. Meriwether may have helped make camp each night. He probably helped hunt, and fished in streams along the way.

WILDERNESS EDUCATION

Georgia was wilderness country and Meriwether loved learning frontier skills. Jefferson wrote about Meriwether going out alone at night to hunt when he was only eight years old.[2] Family legend had nine-year-old Meriwether crossing a field with a group of friends when a bull rushed them. Many of the boys scattered, but Meriwether calmly raised his rifle to shoot at it.

Meriwether wanted to know everything about the plants and animals around him. His mother, a respected herbalist and healer, was delighted with his curiosity. He often asked her questions about the herbs and wild plants she used for cooking and for medicine. These skills helped him identify new plants and treat medical problems on the western expedition.

One of the adults in the Georgia settlement taught Meriwether to read and write. Meriwether loved the wilderness but he wanted a formal education. His mother agreed to send him back to Virginia when he was about thirteen years old. He would go to school and prepare to manage his father's large estate. His guardian, Nicholas Meriwether, managed his inheritance. His inheritance included a 2,000-acre plantation, 24 slaves, 147 gallons of whiskey, and 520 pounds sterling in cash. (British currency was still used in the thirteen colonies).

In eighteenth-century Virginia, planters' sons boarded with their teachers. These teachers were usually preachers or parsons. The teachers' homes were crowded with students. The young men of Meriwether's age studied Latin, English grammar, mathematics, geography, and natural science. But Meriwether soon wrote a letter to his younger brother Reuben, "I should like very much to have some of your Sport, fishing, and hunting."[3]

Jefferson described Meriwether Lewis as an "attentive farmer, observing with minute attention all plants and insects he met with."[4] He added many tracts of land to his holdings. African-American slaves did the hardest work. They built his fences and tilled his crops while overseers supervised them. Virginia planters had time on weekends and holidays to ride beautiful horses on hunts for fox, deer, and bear. They spent their free evenings at dinners and balls.

BORN TO ROAM

Eighteen-year-old Meriwether Lewis had "fits of depression" or "melancholia" like his father. He felt restless and dreamed of traveling. In 1792, he volunteered for a western expedition planned by Secretary of State Thomas Jefferson. But Jefferson felt Lewis was too young to lead an expedition.

In 1794, Lewis volunteered in a militia called up by President George Washington to quell the Whiskey Rebellion in western Pennsylvania. The U.S. government had placed a tax on liquor three years before. It created financial hardship for small farmers in the western counties of states south of New York, from Pennsylvania to Georgia. These westerners protested and refused to pay the tax for three years. Some of them organized an armed rebellion.

The Virginia militia marched to Pittsburgh. The rebellion ended in October 1794. Lewis decided to stay in the military. In 1795, he earned a promotion in rank and transferred to the regular U.S. Army. He served there for six months as an ensign under Lieutenant William Clark in the Chosen Rifle

Company. In 1796, Lewis transferred to the First U.S. Infantry Regiment. He then briefly commanded an infantry company in 1797 at Fort Pickering on the Mississippi River. In 1799, he was promoted to lieutenant, and in 1800, to captain. Lewis had the qualities of a leader. His actions showed him to be brave, resourceful, prudent, and reliable.[5]

Lewis's army life satisfied his need for travel and adventure. Meanwhile, William Clark's life took a similar path.

⬤ THE CLARKS' RIVER JOURNEY WEST

The first two children of John and Ann Rogers Clark were born in a log house on a 410-acre tract in Albemarle County, Virginia. Like the Lewises, the Clarks lived near the hilltop where Jefferson built his estate. They moved east to Virginia's Caroline County to avoid conflict with American Indians. They lived near the road from Fredericksburg to Richmond. William, called Billy, was born there on August 1, 1770. He was the youngest son and the ninth of ten children.[6]

The Clark home was a popular gathering spot for their extended family, friends, and neighbors. Parties, dances, and family gatherings were an important part of their life. The family also valued books and learning. The Clarks made sure their children had a well-rounded education.[7]

Frontier opportunities also tempted William's father as people's optimism returned after the Revolutionary War. He picked up and moved from Caroline County after thirty years of plantation life. In late October 1784, he left his Virginia farm and took the rest of his family and a dozen slaves to Kentucky.

It is unknown how fourteen-year-old William felt about leaving the only home he had ever known. But if he was like his father, brothers, and

Lewis volunteered in a militia called up by President George Washington to stop the Whiskey Rebellion in Pennsylvania. Washington, on the white horse, reviews his militia in October 1794.

other Americans, he probably welcomed new opportunities. The Clarks' African-American slaves had no choice about moving, either. The Clarks and their slaves suffered many hardships along the way, while herding livestock through hilly country on poor roads, in good weather and bad.

The Clarks joined a caravan heading north through Maryland and Pennsylvania. The family traveled across the Blue Ridge and Allegheny mountains. They sailed down the Monongahela and Ohio rivers. The trip became a long four-month journey when winter weather froze the Ohio River. They had to wait until mid-February to continue downriver. William had fun seeing new country. He enjoyed watching the boatmen guide the bulky flatboat with his family's supplies and livestock on board. He did not know he would one day "earn a reputation as an expert waterman."[8]

ROUGH AND READY

After finally reaching Kentucky, the Clarks found a thriving town in Louisville. It had a new court-house and more than one hundred log cabins and clapboard houses, which were constructed with overlapping planks. A log home waited for the Clark family on the south fork of Beargrass Creek.

Life was not easy the first few years for the new westerners. John Clark had to borrow money to buy cattle and supplies. There were problems with American Indians. William's older brother George was ill. While he slowly recovered, George taught William everything he knew about wilderness survival skills.

There were very few schools and tutors on the Kentucky frontier. Many children were often homeschooled. William learned trigonometry, astronomy, navigation, geometry, architecture, and land surveying. He was bright and read many books, but he never mastered written language. Later, his Corps of Discovery journal entries had odd grammar. They also had wildly inconsistent capitalization and spelling. He made up for his poor writing on the expedition with his skills as a draftsman and cartographer.

By the time he was eighteen years old, William Clark seemed ready to tackle anything. People knew him as honest, well-mannered, and eager to please. The sociable and polite young man took his older brothers' troubles, lessons, and their tales of the Revolutionary War to heart. He later put these qualities to use as a negotiator with American Indians.

In 1788, Kentuckians were pleased with the ratification of the U.S. Constitution. They were also happy with the election of President George Washington. They thought a strong government would stop American Indian raids along the Ohio River. But Wea and Miami raiders returned to battle the following spring. The U.S. government engaged in many wars with American Indian nations who aligned with the British. The British hoped to slow the growth of the United States. They wanted to control the fur trade on the Ohio River. Soon the United States would challenge the British in the Pacific Northwest fur trade.

In 1789, nineteen-year-old William Clark volunteered for the Kentucky militia. He had his first experience with Indians and military life on Major John Hardin's expedition to Wea towns. In 1791, Clark became a lieutenant in the regular army. His unit joined the campaign of General Anthony Wayne's Legion. Wayne hoped to end all Indian conflict on the northwestern frontier. In 1794, at the Battle of Fallen Timbers, Wayne defeated American Indians in the Ohio Valley. This battle allowed the U.S. to gain territory as far west as the Mississippi River.

In 1795, Wayne signed the Treaty of Fort Greenville with the region's tribes. By that time, both Lewis and Clark served in Wayne's army as officers. Lewis served as an ensign under Clark. The soldiers became friends.

In 1796, Clark resigned his commission in the army and moved back home. When his father died in 1799, he managed his father's estate. He also tried to help his brother George negotiate lawsuits that traders and merchants brought against him.

He helped pay some of his brother's debt. He took title to thousands of acres George had claimed along the lower Ohio River.

Clark also dreamed of building a canal on the Ohio River at Clarksville. But Meriwether Lewis invited him to join Jefferson's western expedition by the time a company was organized.[9]

JEFFERSON'S WESTERN DREAM

Thomas Jefferson dreamed about exploring the West long before he became president. In 1786, he encouraged John Ledyard's idea to explore North America from west to east. The Connecticut man planned to sail to Alaska from Siberia. Then he would travel through the Northwest into the Mississippi Valley. Ledyard's trip had just started when the Russian police arrested him and then deported him to Poland.

In 1790, Secretary of War Henry Knox tried to start another expedition. He hired Lieutenant John Armstrong to explore the Missouri River. But Armstrong was underprepared. He stopped his expedition at St. Genevieve on the banks of the Mississippi.

Meanwhile, British navigators explored the mouth of the Columbia River. Great Britain had claimed all the land drained by the river and its tributaries. Then another candidate for a U.S. expedition was found. Andre Michaux, a French

Thomas Jefferson became president of the United States in 1801. However, his dream of westward expansion began long before that.

botanist, drew up an agreement for exploration with Philadelphia's American Philosophical Society. But Michaux was a secret agent. France wanted to raise a force to attack Spanish land holdings west of the Mississippi. Jefferson insisted the French government call Michaux back to France.

EXPLORATION FEVER

In 1801, when Jefferson became president, the new nation was a cluster of sixteen states. These states lay between the Atlantic Ocean and the Mississippi River. England, France, and Spain had also claimed parts of North America as their territories. Jefferson knew the United States had to challenge these foreign claims in order to expand.

Jefferson hired twenty-nine-year-old Captain Meriwether Lewis to serve as his private secretary. The president taught Lewis how to survey land, how to use a sextant, and other skills. Jefferson continued to think about exploring the west.

In the summer of 1802, Jefferson's hopes for an expedition grew. He wanted Lewis to lead the expedition. He asked Lewis to drop his other duties. Jefferson taught Lewis all he knew about geography, natural science, politics, American Indians, and diplomacy. They read books about Pacific coast exploration during the fall and winter.

In January 1803, President Jefferson delivered a message to Congress. He requested that Congress renew the Trading House Act. The measure passed in February. This act authorized the U.S. government to build trading posts along the Mississippi River. Jefferson planned to extend the fur trade west of the Mississippi. He wanted to explore possible water routes to the Northwest.

Jefferson encouraged a U.S. takeover of the British fur trade in the interior of North America at the same time.

Jefferson was interested in natural history and the American Indian cultures of the West. But Congress would not fund a scientific expedition. So Jefferson told Congress that Meriwether Lewis would take ten or twelve men on a diplomatic mission. They would attract Canadian furs to the U.S. market. He took care to mention it would only cost the taxpayers $2,500.

"FIXING FOR A START"

Meriwether Lewis drew up a list of supplies for the expedition. In March 1803, he arrived in Harpers Ferry, Virginia (now West Virginia). He began to collect supplies. Lewis's aide in Philadelphia, at his direction, bought some food, tents, tools, kettles, tobacco, corn mills, wine, special uniforms made of drab cloth, gunpowder, and medical and surgical supplies. He also bought and packed hundreds of pounds of gifts and trade goods for American Indians. He packed things such as beads, mirrors, calico shirts, and twists of tobacco.

In Harpers Ferry, Lewis bought rifles from the military arsenal, and stocked up on other tools and necessities. He had an idea for a portable boat frame, and supervised craftsmen in its construction. The frame could be covered with animal

Captain Lewis, at right, inspecting weapons and supplies in Harpers Ferry, Virginia, in 1803.

hides and sealed if another boat was needed when the Corps could not make dugout canoes. With his own money, he bought an airgun that fired many times without reloading.

Jefferson asked the best American scientists and doctors to teach Lewis. During much of the spring of 1803, Lewis studied in Philadelphia. He met with surveyor and astronomer Andrew Ellicott, physician Benjamin Rush, botanist Dr. Benjamin Smith Barton, mathematician Robert Patterson, and anatomist Dr. Caspar Wistar. Lewis learned about the use of scientific instruments, surveying, and medicine. And he also learned about natural history and Indian ethnology.

The scientists and doctors gave Lewis lists of questions about the West.

On July 2, 1803, Secretary of War Henry Dearborn allotted $2,500 for the expedition. He told commanders at western forts to provide Lewis with manpower and supplies. Both Jefferson and Lewis knew the expedition would cost much more. Jefferson believed the U.S. Army should be active in building the country in peacetime. Lewis figured he could lower costs by using soldiers. Army wages were pretty reasonable and the soldiers' monthly pay and rations were the same no matter where they went.

Lewis felt the expedition needed two commanders. He wrote to his former commanding officer and friend William Clark on June 19, 1803. He asked Clark to be co-captain. "If therefore there is anything . . . which would induce you to participate with me in it's fatiegues, it's dangers and it's honors, believe me there is no man on earth with whom I should feel equal pleasure in sharing them as with yourself."[10]

Clark accepted the invitation "with much pleasure." He agreed to join his friend in the "dangers, difficulties, and fatigues" of the journey. "I do assure you that no man lives whith whome I would prefur to undertake Such a Trip," Clark wrote.[11] But a mix-up in Washington would not allow Clark to have a captain's commission. The pair hid

Clark's lower rank from their men and shared the command equally throughout the journey.

In July 1803, President Jefferson sent Robert Livingston and James Monroe to Paris. He wanted them to purchase New Orleans from France. French leader Napoleon not only sold New Orleans, he sold the entire Louisiana Territory to the United States for $15 million. Secretary of War Henry Dearborn acted quickly. He gave Lewis permission to choose volunteers for the western expedition on the same day. The news about doubling the country's size added to the July 4 celebration that year.

Chapter 3
An Epic Journey

On July 5, 1803, Captain Lewis left Washington. After picking up the supplies in Harpers Ferry and Philadelphia, Lewis hired a wagon and driver to take the load of goods overland to Pittsburgh. He supervised construction of the expedition keelboat in Pittsburgh.

At some point that summer, Lewis also purchased a single-masted, flat-bottomed boat. Rowed with seven oars, it was called by the French name, "pirogue."[1] The Corps used two pirogues on the Missouri River. The larger, which may have been the one Lewis purchased first, was painted red; the smaller one was white. Like the keelboat, the pirogues could be rowed, poled, paddled, or sailed.[2] While he waited for the keelboat to be finished, Lewis also purchased a big Newfoundland dog he named Seaman.

On August 31, 1803, the keelboat was completed. Lewis began his journey down the Ohio River. Only George Shannon and John Colter became part of the permanent expedition out of all the hired men and soldiers recruited for the first leg of the expedition. On October 14, 1803, the group on the keelboat arrived in

Clarksville, Indiana. Lewis picked up Captain Clark, his African-American slave York, and the volunteers Clark had recruited: Sergeant Charles Floyd, brothers Joseph and Reuben Field, and George Gibson. The captains called these volunteers the "young men from Kentucky." John Colter officially enlisted on October 15, George Shannon and John Shields enlisted on October 19, and William Bratton and Sergeant Nathaniel Hale Pryor on October 20.[3]

The crew left Clarksville on October 26, 1803. They arrived at Fort Massac on the Illinois bank of the Ohio on November 11.[4] Lewis hired frontiersman George Drouillard as an interpreter. The half-French and half-Shawnee man would become one of the best hunters and woodsmen of the Corps. The Corps grew with the first active-duty U.S. military volunteers: John Newman and Joseph Whitehouse of the 1st Infantry Regiment.

The Corps left Fort Massac on November 13 and arrived near present-day Cairo, Illinois, the next day. Lewis and Clark worked together to describe the geography at the confluence of the Mississippi and Ohio rivers. They learned more about surveying instruments and astronomical calculations. They also measured and compared the speed of the currents and the volume of the two rivers. The captains began to use their diplomatic skills when they met with Delaware and Shawnee chiefs on November 16, 1803.

The crew reached the army post at Kaskaskia, Illinois, on November 28. Six more soldiers enlisted from the 1st U.S. Infantry Regiment: Sergeant John Ordway and Privates Peter M. Weiser, Richard Windsor, Patrick Gass, John Boley, and John Collins. John Dame, John Robertson, Ebeneezer Tuttle, Issac White, and Alexander Hamilton Willard of the U.S. Corps of Artillery also enlisted for the journey. Francois Labiche, another French/Indian man, enlisted with the expedition on November 30. The expedition may have picked up a second boat, the "white pirogue," at Kaskaskia. Orders stated that the Captains were to have the use of "the best boat at the Post."[5]

The idea that a dozen men could make the journey safely for so little money was not realistic. American Indian opposition to American exploration was strong along the Missouri River. The Omaha, Teton Sioux, Arikara, and a few other tribes sometimes "pillaged, blackmailed, and killed traders."[6] These facts were not well known in the East. Lewis did not learn about this problem until he reached St. Louis in late 1803.

WINTER AT CAMP RIVER DUBOIS

Captain Clark established Camp River DuBois, also called Camp Wood. It sat at the confluence of the Mississippi, Missouri, and DuBois rivers north of St. Louis. Clark recruited and trained more men. Lewis took care of paperwork, and then traveled to St. Louis to talk to traders about the upper Missouri regions. He obtained maps made by earlier explorers. He also sent maps, reports, plants, and rocks back to Jefferson in Washington, D.C.

In February 1804, Captain Clark picked a crew of French voyageurs, also called engagés, to man the red pirogue and control the bow of the keelboat. Six soldiers would man the white pirogue.[7] In addition to the eleven men they selected before, in March 1804, the captains enlisted these men into the Corps' permanent party: Sergeant John Ordway, Corporal Richard Warfington, and Privates Patrick Gass, John Boley, John Collins, John Dame, Robert Frazer, Silas Goodrich, Hugh Hall, Thomas Howard, Hugh McNeal, John Potts, Moses Reed, John Robertson, John Thompson, Ebenezer Tuttle, Peter Weiser, William Werner, Issac White, Alexander Willard, and Richard Windsor.

A few soldiers and engagés were well educated, but most had little formal schooling. Like Clark's slave York, some could not read or write. But all of them had special skills such as carpentry, gunsmithing and blacksmithing, hunting, and cooking, and practical experience on the frontier.[8]

"Under a Jentle Brease"

On May 14, 1804, Captain Clark and the Corps of Discovery "proceeded on under a jentle brease up the Missouri" on its first leg north.[9] Captain Lewis joined them in St. Charles, Missouri, along with six soldiers and several French boatmen.

Travel on the Missouri River was difficult. The party averaged only fifteen miles per day. Supplies got wet, and guns rusted. The soldiers made many stops to unload, dry, and repack their cargo. Sergeant Charles Floyd became ill and died near present-day Sioux City, Iowa. Historians believe Floyd died of a burst appendix or a severe intestinal infection.[10] He was the only member of the Corps to die on the journey.

The Corps held councils with some American Indian nations as they traveled along the Missouri River. The first councils were with the Oto and Missouri nations. The captains acted as trading representatives and as diplomats. After an exchange of greetings with tribal leaders, the captains got ready for the council. They erected an awning made from the keelboat mainsail. An American flag was unfurled and placed on a pole. The captains wore their full-dress uniforms and had their soldiers march in a parade drill. Lewis delivered a speech. He usually advised the

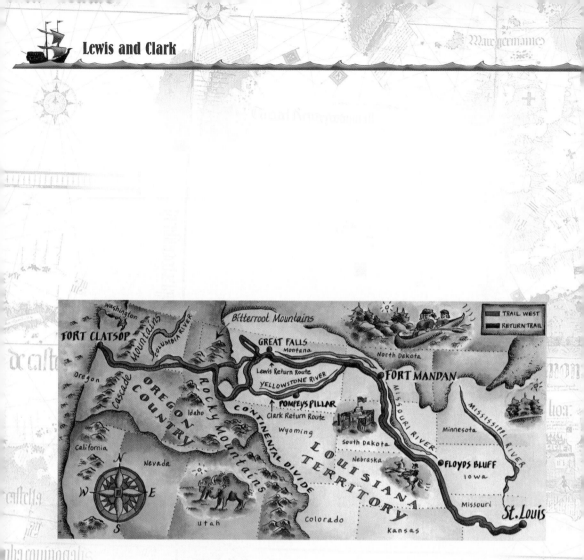

This map shows the routes the Lewis and Clark expedition took to the Pacific Ocean and on their return journey home.

American Indians about the government the Corps was representing: "Children, we have been sent by the great Chief of the Seventeen great nations of America to inform you."[11] Sometimes there was a display of technology like the air gun, magnet, spyglass, compass, and watch. Then the captains gave peace medals with a likeness of President Jefferson, certificates, and other gifts to the most important chiefs.

News of the expedition spread up the Missouri River. Most of the upriver tribes welcomed the expedition. But the Teton Sioux wanted to control all trade on the river. If they could control the flow of European goods to the Arikara, Mandan, and Hidatsa villagers, the Sioux position would be strong. But if the villagers gained access to the St. Louis trade such as the Corps represented, then their power as middlemen would be lost.

President Jefferson wanted the Corps to have a council with the Teton Sioux. "On that nation, we wish most particularly to make a friendly impression because of the immense power, and because we learn they are very desirous of being on the most friendly terms with us," he wrote.[12]

After exchanging food with three bands of the Teton Sioux on September 25, the Corps tried to talk to the Teton Sioux. But French interpreter Pierre Cruzatte spoke little of their language. Lewis gave a shortened version of his speech, and

the soldiers performed their usual parade. As the last gifts were exchanged, a chief of the Brule band felt slighted when the Corps did not give him a gift. A battle between the Sioux and the Corps almost erupted when some young Sioux members seized the pirogue's bow cable. The Corps displayed their superior firepower and a wise chief, Black Buffalo, helped end the tension. He asked the Corps to let the Sioux women and children visit the keelboat. Two days later, there was another clash when the Corps departed to go upriver against the will of the Sioux. Black Buffalo intervened again and allowed both sides to keep their dignity and avoid bloodshed.[13]

WINTER AT FORT MANDAN

The Corps of Discovery reached the Mandan and Hidatsa earth-lodge villages in late October 1804. They built Fort Mandan, near present-day Washburn, North Dakota, and spent the winter of 1804–1805 there. The Captains talked with the Indians and the British and French traders about the terrain and Indian nations that lay ahead. York was a popular curiosity that winter. Le Borgne (One-Eye), a Hidatsa chief, examined York closely. He tried to rub off the "dark paint" from York's body with his moistened fingers. When he looked at York's scalp through his hair, he was convinced York was not painted.

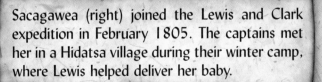

Sacagawea (right) joined the Lewis and Clark expedition in February 1805. The captains met her in a Hidatsa village during their winter camp, where Lewis helped deliver her baby.

The Captains recruited a French interpreter from a Hidatsa village. Toussaint Charbonneau wanted to bring along his young wife, Sacagawea (Bird Woman), and her baby boy, Jean Baptiste. Lewis had helped deliver the baby in February. Clark later nicknamed him Pomp. Lewis and Clark finally agreed to Charbonneau's request. Sacagawea was a Shoshone captured by the Hidatsa. She could still speak Shoshone and would help interpret when they encountered her people. The Mandan, Hidatsa, and Sacagawea informed Lewis and Clark that the Shoshone could provide the horses they would need to travel from the headwaters of the Missouri River over the Rocky Mountains to the Columbia River. Because women with babies did not travel with war parties, her presence would ease Indians' fear of the explorers.

Lewis and Clark sent the keelboat and a small party back to St. Louis on April 7, 1805. The keelboat carried reports, maps, letters, and personal gifts from Clark and York to their families. It also carried a large collection of plant and animal specimens, and American Indian clothing and tools. The soldiers also had to care for a live grouse, four magpies, and a prairie dog.

The remaining thirty-three Corps of Discovery members went upstream in the two pirogues and six dugout canoes.[14] The group headed into country known only to American Indians. No other European or American explorers had ever entered these lands.

ACROSS THE PLAINS

Wild game was abundant as the Corps traveled across the plains of North Dakota. Deer, buffalo (or bison), elk, and antelope were visible in all directions. Lewis and Clark, Drouillard, Charbonneau, Sacagawea, and the baby all began to sleep in a buffalo-skin tepee. The hunters also found many beaver, one of the principal furs used for hats in the East. In mid-April, the Corps met their first grizzly bear as they traveled closer to the mouth of the Yellowstone River.

The Corps passed through the "Breaks of the Missouri" in May 1805. Many bighorn sheep lived along the crags and cliffs. The river shoals and rapids became more dangerous. Towering sandstone cliffs hemmed in the expedition on the river for two weeks. Before this point, Captain Lewis had walked along the shore to study plants and wildlife, and the hunters had ranged away from the water. But now everyone had to stay in the boats. Lewis and Clark hiked separately up the sandstone bluffs on May 26 and viewed snowy mountain crests in the distance. They mistakenly thought the mountains were the main range of the Rockies.

A Major Fork

On June 1, 1805, the Corps reached a major fork in the river. The Captains had to decide which was the Missouri. If they made the wrong decision, they would lose time and not cross the Rockies before winter. The right decision would lead them to the Rockies, the Shoshone, and horses. The wrong fork would take them into the territory of the hostile Blackfeet. It took a week for the men to explore the forks and to decide to take the south fork as the Missouri River.

They knew from the Hidatsa's descriptions they were close to the Great Falls of the Missouri. Lewis and a small party set out from the forks toward the Falls. Clark and the main party followed the next day with all the boats except the red pirogue. They had cached—hidden—the pirogue, equipment, and supplies along the riverbank.

The explorers spent a month at the Great Falls, portaging their canoes and equipment around the five waterfalls at Great Falls after crossing most of present-day Montana. The Hidatsa had mentioned only one fall. After the portage, Lewis tried to use the collapsible boat he had built at Harpers Ferry. But he did not have pitch to seal the animal skins. The mixtures he made from buffalo tallow, beeswax, and pounded charcoal did not work well. The disappointed Lewis and his men buried

After portaging around the Great Falls of the Missouri River, Lewis tried to use the collapsible boat he had built at Harpers Ferry. This artist's rendering shows from left to right: Lewis, Patrick Gass, and John Shields stretching leather skins around the frame.

"the experiment." It took five days to make two new dugout canoes.[15]

CAMP FORTUNATE

Sacagawea began to recognize the countryside beyond the Great Falls. She assured the Corps they would soon meet her people, the Shoshone, who had many horses. On August 8, she recognized Beaverhead Rock and told the Corps it was not far from the summer retreat of the Shoshone. On August 9, Captain Lewis and three men scouted seventy-five miles ahead of the expedition's main party, crossing the Continental Divide at present-day Lemhi Pass. They saw a young Shoshone man on a horse who evaded them. On August 13, they found a woman and two young girls who led them toward their camp. Eventually, the two parties reunited and made a new camp. They stayed in Camp Fortunate until August 24.

The first order of business was food for the hungry Corps, and then a council with Chief Cameahwait. Sacagawea interpreted at the meeting. She had an emotional reunion with the young chief, who she said was her brother. She translated from Shoshone into Hidatsa, Charbonneau translated Hidatsa into French, and Labiche translated French into English. Lewis and Clark made their standard speeches and medal presentations. They told Cameahwait that in order to trade with the

United States he would need to help them with horses and a guide.

Captain Clark and a small party explored the Salmon River during their stay. It was impassable by boat or land, as the Shoshone said. Eventually, the Captains bartered for twenty-nine horses and a mule. Old Toby, the man who guided Clark on the Salmon River, and his three sons agreed to guide them over the Rocky Mountains.

THE BITTERROOT RANGE

The Corps of Discovery turned north on August 30, 1805. The countryside became rugged and their horses sometimes slipped or fell on the slopes in the rain and sleet. On September 4, the Corps climbed a high spur of the Bitterroot Range, moved through a pass and reentered Montana. They encountered Salish Indians living in a village at the base of the Bitterroot Mountains. This place was later called Ross's Hole. They spent two days with the Salish, holding councils and bartering for more horses.

Early on the afternoon of September 6, the expedition headed north. They traveled through the spectacular scenery of the Bitterroot Valley along the Bitterroot River and the saw-toothed Bitterroot Range. They reached Lolo Creek three days later. It would take them along the Lolo Trail and across the Bitterroot Range. They made camp for two days at a spot they called Travelers Rest.

The well-defined trail became very difficult to travel as it wound through high, rocky slopes and deep gorges. Morale sagged. On September 12, Ordway wrote, "we found no water nor place to Camp until 10 oClock at night . . . we could not find a level place to Sleep, and Scarcely any feed for our horses."[16] On September 16, a severe snowstorm started before dawn. By nightfall, the nearly starving group trudged through six to eight inches of new snow. The group killed a colt and ate it along with some "portable soup"—a dried mixture of beans and vegetables that Lewis purchased before the journey. The Corps had to kill two more colts and a horse in the following days to eat.

NEZ PERCE COUNTRY

The Corps finally reached Nez Perce country on the banks of the Clearwater River in present-day Idaho on September 20. At first, the tribe was alarmed by the expedition. Then an old woman, Watkuweis, urged her people not to harm the Corps of Discovery. She had been kidnapped by another tribe and was later treated very kindly by whites.

The Corps feasted with their new hosts on their staple foods—dried salmon, berries, and camas roots, the onion-shaped bulb of the camas lily. Clark warned the Corps not to eat too much food.

The entire expedition became sick for several days. This could have been from the change in diet, bacteria in the fish, or maybe even eating too much food on empty stomachs.

The Corps noted that the Nez Perce had many fine horses. But they were going to travel by river again and needed canoes. The Nez Perce pastured the Corps' horses and showed them how they crafted dugout canoes. Rather than carving out the logs, the Nez Perce put them over a very slow-burning fire trench and burned them out. It took ten days to make four large and one small canoe.

The Corps floated down the Clearwater and Snake rivers along with Nez Perce guides between October 7 and 16. They bought dogs to eat from villages along the river. They also ate fish and roots when little game was available. They saw Yakima, Wanapum, Walla Walla, and other Shahaptian-speaking tribes who had an economy similar to the Nez Perce.

As the Corps proceeded upstream into areas populated by Chinookan tribes, they noticed man-ufactured objects of American or European origin. While some of these trade goods were traded from the east and south, some goods such as scarlet and blue cloth blankets and a sailor's jacket could only have come from NorthWest Company traders. The items were a sign that their journey was almost over. When the wide Columbia River came into

Meriwether Lewis, standing in front of the boat, leads the Corps down the Columbia River. The expedition knew when it reached the Columbia that it was near the Pacific Ocean.

view on October 16, the Corps knew they would soon reach the Pacific Ocean.

THE COLUMBIA WATERSHED

On October 23, 1805, the boats entered a dangerous but beautiful stretch of the Columbia. There were sudden rapids and drops as the stream tore its way through the Cascade Range on a sharp descent to the sea. It took more than a week of combined portage and navigation with poles and cords to get through the fifty-five-mile stretch.

The expedition met new Chinook-speaking tribes whose lives depended on salmon fishing. They traveled by water because thick forests made travel and hunting by horse difficult. Many lower-river Chinook Indians were friendly and cooperative. Others, however, were tricky traders and thieves. The Indians in the Celilo Falls-Dalles-Cascades area harassed the Corps. The slow travel on the river gave them the chance to rob travelers. The expedition's size, superior weaponry, and special security measures prevented major problems. But the two Nez Perce guides, Tetoharsky and Twisted Hair, returned home because they could no longer be of service as interpreters.

The Corps emerged from the Columbia River gorge and left the Cascade Mountains behind. Between October 25 and early November, the

Corps made contact with a number of Chinookan people. They often stopped at villages to purchase dogs and dried fish to eat. Because of the language barrier, they did not have long councils but they did distribute medals and gifts to the village leaders. Already accustomed to European traders and goods, the Chinookan tribes enjoyed York and Cruzatte's fiddle music.

On November 2, the Corps saw that the river was more than two miles wide at Beacon Rock, the beginning of tidewater. Game and waterfowl began to appear. Mount Hood, which they first sighted on October 18, was in view again on November 3. The Corps noted more European goods, such as guns, swords, clothing, and copper and brassware, among the Chinookan-speaking Skilloots near present-day Portland, Oregon, and Vancouver, Washington.

"Ocian in View! O! The Joy"

On November 7, 1805, Clark wrote, "Great joy in camp we are in view of the Ocian, this great Pacific Octean which we been So long anxious to See."[17] But he was looking at the estuary of the Columbia. Its salty waters reached twenty miles inland. The rain that started on November 5 continued for eleven straight days. High waves and heavy winds tossed the canoes around like toys. The Corps members were wet, miserable, and tired from bailing water out of the boats. Clothing, bedding, and equipment became soaked. Sacagawea and some of the men were seasick. Huge cedar, fir, and spruce tree trunks up to two hundred feet long and seven feet in diameter surged around in the river. Clark wrote on November 12, "It would be distressing to a feeling person to See our Situation at this time all wet and cold . . . in a Cove Scercely large enough to Contain us."[18]

Hunting was impossible. The Corps bought dried fish, roots, and dogs from the Chinook almost daily. Shelter was hard to find and fires were very tough to start. But the expedition had to stop and camp on November 10–15. Then they moved downstream about five miles and established another camp near an abandoned Chinook village. From the Corps' camp in today's Wahkiakum County, Washington, they could finally look west to the mouth of the Columbia and the Pacific Ocean. They used the new camp as a main base for the next ten days.

After many months of hard work, the journey west was over. Clark estimated their distance from Camp River DuBois at 4,133 miles. Lewis and Clark ventured out with small parties to explore the area, including Cape Disappointment, the Pacific Ocean, and the long sandy beaches. Both captains and their men carved their names and the dates on trees at least twice to prove that U.S. military officers had reached the Pacific Coast by land. They traded with the Chinook, who often wanted more for their roots, salmon, and berries than the Corps could offer.

WINTER AT FORT CLATSOP

Lewis and Clark knew they could not return up the Columbia River and over the mountains until spring came. They scouted a location for a winter camp. All members of the expedition, including Sacagawea and York, voted on possible locations. In December 1805, the Corps of Discovery built Fort Clatsop on the south side of the Columbia River near present-day Astoria, Oregon. The Clatsop said elk and roots were in good supply there. The Corps became friends with a Clatsop chief, Coboway, who liked to visit the fort.

Most of the men moved into the fort after a frantic effort to finish the roof during a heavy rain on Christmas Eve. Clark's journal entries during the week after Christmas begin with "rained last night as usual," "rained and blew hard last night," or "rained and blew with great Violence."[19] The captains recorded as much as they could about the Pacific coast and its people, despite the rainy winter weather and their bad moods. Most of the men's wool clothing had worn out and their leather clothing was rotting from the damp air.

Many of the men were sick. Everyone complained about the depressing weather, infestations of fleas and lice, and boredom.

The captains did all they could to keep everyone busy. They assigned a rotating detail of three men to make salt for the return trip by boiling seawater on the beach. The rest of the men had to dress elk hides to make clothes and moccasins. By March 13, they had finished about ten pairs of moccasins per person. The moccasins wore out quickly under the hard traveling conditions.

Between December 1, 1805, and March 20, 1806, the Corps bagged 131 elk, twenty deer, a few beaver and otter, and one raccoon. They supplemented their diet with some fish. They exhausted the game in the area and had to range out as far as twenty miles to hunt. They continued to buy berries, roots, dried fish, and dogs from local area tribes. Captain Clark was the only Corps member who would not eat dog.

One event that broke up the group's boredom was a thirty-mile jaunt to see the carcass of a whale. It had washed ashore near the salt camp. Sacagawea insisted on going along. On January 6, Clark wrote:

> The last evening Shabono [Charbonneau] and his Indian woman was very impatient to be permitted to go with me, and was therefore indulged; She observed that She had traveled a long way with us

to See the great waters, and that now that [the] monstrous fish was also to be Seen, She thought it verry hard that She Could not be permitted to See either (She had never yet been to the Ocian).[20]

Clark allowed Sacagawea, Jean Baptiste, and Charbonneau to join him and eleven other men on the trip. The Tillamook Indians had stripped the whale of its meat and blubber. But Clark was able to purchase three hundred pounds and a few gallons of rendered oil.

All winter long, the Corps watched for English or American northwest traders. The expedition needed more trade goods. Jefferson said the Corps had the option to sail back to the east coast if they chose. But most traders came in April and traded their goods for furs until October or November. Captain Samuel Hill, commander of the brig *Lydia* out of Boston, traded along the mouth of the Columbia for a few weeks in November 1805. But neither he nor the Corps were aware of one another's presence.

Everyone grew restless as winter ended. Lewis and Clark wanted to cross the Lolo Trail with the Nez Perce in the spring. The chiefs had told them they intended to cross to the eastern side of the mountains as early as possible. If the Corps did not meet them, they could not reclaim their horses and might have trouble crossing the Bitterroot Mountains on their own.

One of the captains' final chores was to write and post lists of the names of men in the Corps. Included on the back was a sketched map of the Upper Missouri and Columbia rivers and the expedition routes. The captains gave these notices to Coboway and other chiefs. One was posted in the captains' room at Fort Clatsop. They hoped a northwest trader might find a notice if something happened to them on the way home. Then the world would know about their accomplishments. When Captain Hill returned in the spring of 1806 after trading farther up the coast, some American Indians gave his crew peace medals that Lewis and Clark had presented to them, and a notice the explorers had left behind.[21]

On March 22, 1806, the captains sent out an advance hunting party and said goodbye to Chief Coboway. They gave Fort Clatsop and its furniture to him. The next morning was wet and cloudy, just like the departure from Camp River DuBois in 1804. The men loaded their three large and three small canoes and paddled down the Columbia River, beginning their return journey home.

Chapter 4

HEADING HOME

The Corps members endured bad weather, high water, and strong currents on the Columbia again. They had problems with vandalism and theft by Chinookan Indians living along the river. Captain Lewis eventually lost his temper. He struck one Indian and kicked him out of camp. On April 11, 1806, three Indians from a Chinookan tribe lured Lewis's dog away. Lewis sent three of his men to chase the thieves. They recovered the dog.

On the trip home, Clark and a small party explored the Willamette River. They went inland ten miles to the site of today's city of Portland. The American Indians they met were starving. They had used their winter store of food and the salmon run would not start until May. Captain Clark wrote, "This information gives us much uneasiness with respect to our future means of Subsistence."[1]

At the Dalles, the Corps sold some of their canoes and chopped others into firewood. Instead of fighting the rough water, they bought and rented horses to carry their equipment and supplies. They used an overland shortcut between the Columbia and the Clearwater. The shortcut took them around most of the Snake River and saved them about eighty miles.

In early May, the Corps arrived in Nez Perce territory and found their old friends Tetoharsky and Twisted Hair. Twisted Hair had agreed to care for the soldiers' horses. But when he helped guide the Corps to the Columbia River, other chiefs had to watch the horses. They quarreled about the chore, and some of the horses ran away. The Corps was able to retrieve about half of their saddles and twenty-one horses.

RECROSSING THE BITTERROOTS

Lewis and Clark were concerned when the Nez Perce said it was too early to cross the Bitterroots. The snow was deep and there was no grass for the horses yet. On May 10, the Corps established their camp near a Nez Perce village in present-day Kamiah, Idaho. They stayed in Camp Chopunnish for a month.

Shortage of food was a problem. Both the Corps and the Nez Perce had to resort to eating horses. Clark stayed busy distributing salves, laxatives, and eyewash, and other medicines. He attended to injuries and ailments as he had at many American Indian settlements. The Corps used the time to relax and socialize with the Nez Perce. They held foot and horse races, and Cruzatte played his fiddle for many dances.

On June 10, Lewis and Clark moved from Camp Chopunnish to a location near the Lolo Trail. They traveled northeast about eight miles to where they had first met the Nez Perce. On June 15, the expedition set out over the Lolo Trail without guides. But the Corps had started too early. As they ascended into the mountains, the snow became deep. The trail was visible at times only because the Nez Perce had peeled the outer bark from trees to obtain the inner bark for food. The group's horses often slipped on the steep and icy path. The expedition became short of food.

On the morning of June 17, Lewis and Clark decided to turn back. The men cached most of the baggage, a little food, and the instruments and papers high in some trees. Still hopeful, they sent Drouillard and George Shannon ahead to the Nez Perce villages to hire guides. On June 21, the exhausted Corps arrived back at the camp on Weippe Prairie. Two days later, Drouillard and Shannon brought in three young Nez Perce who agreed to serve as guides.

Undaunted by its bad experience, the Corps set out with the new guides. They recovered the cache on the mountain two days later. The snow was about half as deep as before. On June 28, the

expedition passed the point where Old Toby had mistakenly gone the year before. The next day, the Corps found the route and passed into present-day Montana from Idaho. They stopped at Lolo Hot Springs to bathe and relax in the steaming water. On June 30, they arrived back in Travelers Rest. It took just six days to travel what had taken eleven days on the trip west.

EXPLORING THE MARIAS AND YELLOWSTONE

The Captains made plans at Fort Clatsop for the Corps to explore the Marias and the Yellowstone Rivers. From Travelers Rest, the Corps would break into groups with separate missions. Lewis would travel with nine men and seventeen horses over a buffalo route to the Great Falls of the Missouri. Three of his men would dig up the cache there and prepare for portage. With the other six volunteers, he would explore the Upper Marias. Then he would go to the mouth of the Marias and meet the men coming down the Missouri.

In the meantime, Sergeant Pryor would travel with Clark and the main group to the head of the Jefferson River, where the Corps had left its canoes before crossing the Lemhi Pass with the Shoshone. Ordway and a party of ten men would descend the Jefferson and the Missouri in the canoes. The three men left by Lewis would help

After crossing the Bitterroot range of the Rocky Mountains, the Corps of Discovery explored different parts of the Missouri River valley. This is a view of the Missouri River valley.

with the portage around the falls. After the portage, the fourteen men would go to the mouth of the Marias and join Lewis and his party. Then the combined group would meet Clark and his group after they had explored the Yellowstone. At the junction of the Missouri and the Yellowstone, almost the entire Corps would come together again. Sergeant Pryor and two privates would take the horses to the Mandan villages and try to deliver a message from Lewis to Hugh Heney, a Canadian trader. Lewis wanted Heney to persuade

some Sioux chiefs to join the expedition and visit Washington.

On July 3, 1806, the parties started out from Travelers Rest. They would separate for forty days, until August 12. Only part of the plan worked out. Dividing the group caused morale to fall. Clark's party worried about Lewis's party, which had traveled into hostile Blackfeet territory.

Lewis and his men saw abandoned Blackfeet camps along the way. The five Nez Perce guides would not go any farther on July 4. On July 7, Lewis crossed the Continental Divide, back into Louisiana Territory through a pass near present-day Helena, Montana. Settlers later named it Lewis and Clark Pass. Clark and the main party crossed the divide at Gibbons Pass.

When Lewis reached the Great Falls of the Missouri, his men opened the upper portage cache to find water had damaged it. They dug up the old portage wagon wheels and the experimental boat frame. Those were in better shape. Just before they reached the Great Falls, they lost seven horses to Blackfeet raiders. With fewer horses, they had to break up into smaller groups in order to handle the latest portage of canoes and baggage. They also had to recover the white pirogue and supplies hidden at the lower portage camp.

Lewis, Drouillard, and the Field brothers stayed at Camp Disappointment from July 22 to

July 26, 1806. There were some signs of Blackfeet warriors in the area. On July 26, Lewis decided to meet the rest of the party.

SCRAPPING WITH THE BLACKFEET

Lewis and the Field brothers climbed the river bluffs and Drouillard hiked into the valley to hunt. When Lewis reached the top, he saw eight American Indians and about thirty horses on the bluffs a mile away. They seemed to be watching Drouillard. In spite of his concerns, Lewis approached the men. They were Piegan, one of the Blackfeet's three main bands. The two groups greeted each other and smoked a pipe.

As was his custom, Lewis gave one young man a medal, another a flag, and the third a handkerchief. The two groups agreed to camp down below on the Two Medicine River. Lewis told them how the U.S. government wanted to establish peace between all tribes and trade with all American Indian nations in the West. The Blackfeet erected a large buffalo-skin tent. Lewis and Drouillard accepted an invitation to sleep inside the tent. The Field brothers decided to stay outside.

Lewis and the Blackfeet shared more information with Drouillard as interpreter. The Blackfeet talked about their tribe, their hunting excursions, and their trading. Lewis spoke about the Corps'

journey and the government's work to bring peace and commercial trade to the tribes.

All went well until dawn. The Blackfeet crowded around the fire. Joseph Field left his rifle near where his brother Reuben slept. An Indian slipped behind Joseph and grabbed the brothers' rifles. Two others crept into the tent and took Drouillard's and Lewis's rifles.

The Field brothers chased the man who carried their weapons. They overtook him. Reuben plunged a knife into his heart. When Drouillard and Captain Lewis awakened to the commotion, Lewis chased the other thief with a pistol. He motioned to him to lay the rifle down. The Field brothers and Droulliard wanted to shoot him. Lewis said it was against their orders to harm an American Indian unless their lives were in grave danger. The man dropped the rifles and walked away.

U.S. trade with their enemies, especially of weapons, would threaten the Blackfeet nation's way of life. The young men decided to steal the Corps' horses. Captain Lewis ordered his men to shoot if necessary. Drouillard and the Field brothers chased the largest group of Blackfeet who tried to drive some horses upriver. Lewis pursued two others who were also trying to herd horses away. These two turned into a ravine about nine hundred feet from camp. One jumped behind a rock. The other turned and faced Captain Lewis. Lewis shot him in the abdomen and he died.

Captain Lewis returned to camp because he could not reload his rifle. Drouillard met him on the way. The Field brothers recovered four of their six horses. They abandoned one of their own horses and took four Blackfeet horses. They saddled and packed the horses as fast as they could. They burned the scattered Blackfeet possessions, except for a gun and some buffalo meat. Lewis also repossessed the flag he had given to one of the Indians. But he left the medal around the neck of another so the tribe "might be informed who we are."[2]

ON THE RUN

Lewis's party covered sixty-three miles by mid-afternoon and made another seventeen miles by dark. They stopped for two hours to eat. Then they traveled another twenty miles. At 2 A.M., the party stopped to sleep and let the horses graze.[3] The men struggled into the saddle again at daybreak on July 28. Their lives depended on their quick movement. After twelve miles, they realized they were near the Missouri River. The men thought they heard the sound of a gun. Eight miles later, they heard the unmistakable sound of rifle fire above the mouth of the Marias.

When they ran to the riverbank, they saw Sergeant Gass, Sergeant Ordway, and their boat party.[4]

Captain Lewis and his companions had ridden one-hundred and twenty miles in slightly more than twenty-four hours. They stripped their equipment from their horses, turned them loose, and then cast off in the boats. The increased manpower and weaponry would help if a war party caught up. About noon that day, the reunited party arrived at the mouth of the Marias. After looking around for Blackfeet, they opened the main cache and several smaller ones on the riverbank. The main cache had caved in and damaged the bulk of the contents. The small caches were in good order. In the early afternoon, Sergeant Gass and Private Willard arrived with the horses from the Great Falls. Everyone moved to the small island at the mouth of the river where they had hidden the red pirogue. It had decayed beyond repair, but they salvaged the nails and iron parts.

When the group reached the mouth of the Yellowstone on August 7, Captain Clark was not there. They found a tattered note attached to a pole at an old campsite. Game was scarce and mosquitoes were plentiful. Captain Lewis and his men went farther downriver to look for Clark's party.

Many things went wrong on Lewis's trip, and very little was accomplished. Clark and his party returned to Camp Fortunate at the forks of the Beaver River. They retrieved the supplies and canoes cached there. They washed and repaired the canoes, and Sergeant Ordway and his crew headed downriver to the Great Falls. Clark and his party of twelve explored the Yellowstone on horseback. They awaited the arrival of Captain Lewis and his men when they reached the junction of the Yellowstone and the Missouri rivers. Clark was surprised when Sergeant Pryor and his party came from upriver in a Mandan-style "buffalo boat" they had made from buffalo hide. American Indian raiders had stolen their horses and they could not reach the Mandan villages.

●LEWIS AND CLARK REUNITE

On August 11, Pierre Cruzatte accidentally shot Lewis in the hip and buttock as they were hunting elk. On the morning of August 12, Lewis's party met two American trappers, Joseph Dickson and Forrest Hancock. The trappers said they had passed the Clark party the day before. Lewis and his crew pushed hard to catch up. At about 1 P.M. on August 12, Captain Lewis's party finally caught up with Captain Clark's party. "I over took Capt. Clark and party and had the pleasure of finding them all well."[5] Clark was alarmed to find Lewis wounded and lying in the white pirogue. Each

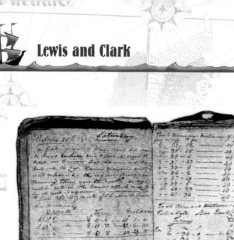

These are pages from William Clark's diary of the 1804–1806 expedition. Clark explored the Yellowstone River with his party while Lewis explored the Marias River before reuniting near the Mandan villages.

leader of the five parties—Clark, Lewis, Gass, Pryor, and Ordway—compared notes on what had happened to the others during the past six weeks.

The entire group set out that afternoon in the five canoes, the white pirogue, and the two lashed-together canoes that Clark had built on the Upper Yellowstone. Two days later, the Mandan villages came into view.

FAREWELL AT THE MANDAN VILLAGES

The return to the Mandan villages on August 14 marked the end of the trip for Sacagawea, Charbonneau, and their son. They were home.

Clark agreed to release Private Colter from his service. Colter joined Dickson and Hancock's new trapping expedition to the Yellowstone.

Down the Missouri, Captains Lewis and Clark held council with tribes they had visited on the westward journey. They invited Sheheke, a Mandan chief, to travel with them to St. Louis and then to Washington. They also visited and repaired Sergeant Floyd's grave. This was a busy time for the Corps. Lewis and Clark collected more natural histories and drew maps. The men hunted and gathered fruit.

By this time, Captain Lewis had recovered from his wound and could walk again. Unlike the hard trip upstream, the Corps raced downstream, traveling as much as thirty to seventy miles a day. The expedition met and camped with trading parties going upstream nearly every day. Americans were moving into the western frontier before the Corps had even returned. The traders gave the men some biscuits, sugar, flour, pork, chocolate, and tobacco. They listened to the wild rumors that the Corps had been killed by animals or Indians.

On September 20, the sight of cows on the bank near La Charette brought shouts of joy. As the Corps of Discovery landed at the village, trading boats fired rounds to salute them. Citizens provided food, music, and dancing that evening. For a few more nights, they stopped in hospitable

Sacagawea's journey ended at the Mandan villages on August 14, 1806. This George Catlin painting depicts a Mandan Bull Dance.

communities along the river. Celebrations became the explorers' new way of life.

September 23, 1806, was the last day of the epic voyage. The Corps traveled the last few miles of the Missouri River. They crossed the Mississippi and made a quick visit to Camp River DuBois, where they had departed two years, four months, and ten days before. The boats then swept downstream to St. Louis and docked at noon. Nearly everybody in town lined the riverfront to cheer the Corps. The town's leading citizens held a dinner and ball in the Corps of Discovery's honor.

Chapter 5

A Failed Mission?

The Corps of Discovery had traveled more than eight thousand miles in less than two and a half years. Few explorations in history were so free of mistakes and accidents. The Corps lost only one member of their party. They killed two Indians in the single skirmish of the expedition. In the areas of diplomatic relations and gathering scientific data, the expedition was successful by today's standards.

Thomas Jefferson repeatedly said the Corps' most important mission was to find "the most direct and practicable water communication across this continent for the purposes of commerce."[1] The Corps of Discovery failed in that mission. They did not find a direct water route to the Pacific. It is now known that the fabled Northwest Passage does not exist. The Corps of Discovery had not established that fact.

The expedition became a model for army exploration in the West. It also set a pattern for government-sponsored scientific exploration. Lewis and Clark's experiences on the journey were their success. They described land, natural

Lewis and Clark recorded many pages of information about plants, animals, and American Indians that they encountered on their journey. They also drew maps. This is a selection of pages from the journals of Lewis and Clark.

history, and American Indian cultures that were unfamiliar to Western science. They explored four major rivers—the Missouri, the Columbia, the Snake, and the Yellowstone—and their tributaries.

President Jefferson's detailed list of questions to Lewis about natural features and American Indian tribes in the Louisiana Territory is now a classic exploration document. Captains Lewis and Clark recorded many pages of the scientific information that Jefferson requested. Sergeant Charles Floyd, Sergeant John Ordway, Sergeant Patrick Gass, Private Joseph Whitehouse, and Captains Lewis and Clark wrote 1.5 million words about what they observed and experienced on the expedition. The Corps of Discovery's journals, maps, plant and animal specimens, and notes on American Indian societies were like an encyclopedia on the Louisiana Territory.

In 1809, President Jefferson deposited most of the journals with the American Philosophical Society in Philadelphia. William Clark and American diplomat and financier Nicholas Biddle compiled a report about the expedition. The War of 1812 began just as Biddle was ready to turn the volume over to the printer. Biddle published two thousand copies of an abridged, two-volume collection of the journals in 1814. This version, however, left out most of the information about plant and animal life. Naturalists and later explorers and settlers

renamed many of the Corps' natural science and geographic discoveries. The expedition received no credit for most of its natural science discoveries.

Other than the 1814 report and Sergeant Patrick Gass's journal (which was edited and rushed into print in 1807), the expedition journals lay mostly unused and unpublished for a century. In 1904, to commemorate the 100th anniversary of the Corps of Discovery, Dr. Reuben Gold Thwaites edited the original journals. He published them in an eight-volume set. The set included the journals of Lewis and Clark, Sergeant Floyd, and Private Whitehouse. It also included Clark's maps and letters of importance to the story. Not until 1979 did the University of Nebraska publish a new and complete version of the journals.

WESTERN GEOGRAPHY

William Clark was responsible for charting the journey. He became a gifted mapmaker. Lewis recorded astronomical observations to help determine latitude and longitude. Together, they were among the first geographers of the west. Lewis and Clark determined the course of the Upper Missouri and its major tributaries. Before the expedition, maps of the North American continent had an empty interior. They showed a single mountain range as the Continental Divide.

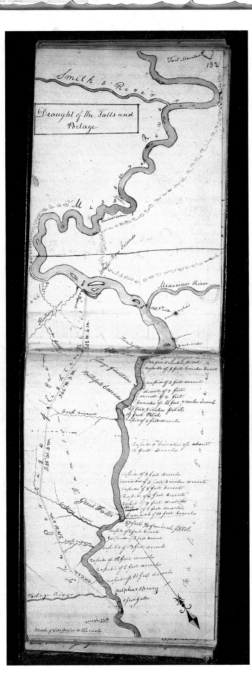

William Clark charted most of the journey and was a gifted mapmaker. Clark drew this map in his journal of the expedition's portatge around the Great Falls of the Missouri.

The Louisiana Purchase and the Lewis and Clark expedition opened up the West to a rush of new settlers. This 1866 lithograph shows a wagon train traveling through the Rocky Mountains.

Captain Clark charted intricate maps with tangles of rivers and mountains. Most important were the three improved maps Clark drew between 1804 and 1810 of the western United States and lower Canada. It would take another fifty years after the expedition for other cartographers to complete an accurate western map. But Clark's map of the West became a useful tool for the settlers who would soon venture into the Louisiana Territory.[2]

NATURAL SCIENCE OF THE WEST

Lewis became the Corps' most skilled naturalist. His descriptions of flowers, trees, fish, reptiles, and mammals are detailed, colorful, and creative. In his last journal entry, on August 12, 1806, Lewis described his gunshot wound in only a few lines. But he described in beautiful detail a cherry tree he observed on the Missouri River bottom lands. In all, Lewis collected, pressed, dried, and returned with more than 240 botanical specimens. The Corps of Discovery described more than 178 plants and 122 animals unknown to science in 1800.[3]

WESTERN ETHNOGRAPHY

Lewis and Clark also became anthropologists as they collected information about the American Indian tribes they encountered. They were careful to note information about Indian languages and cultures. They also collected practical information helpful to establishing trade.

The expedition had a major impact on ethnography. The two captains' descriptions of the American Indians and their way of life contained some errors and misconceptions. But in other

Prairie dogs were one of the many mammals detailed by Lewis in his journals. The Corps also sent a prairie dog back to President Jefferson at the beginning of their journey.

ways, Lewis and Clark were so accurate in their reports that their work became the basis for future ethnologists. Before the expedition, not much was known about Indian nations west of the Mandan villages and along the Upper Columbia River. Lewis and Clark were the first Americans to encounter and describe the Northern Shoshone, Salish, Nez Perce, Cayuse, Yakima, and Walla Walla. The explorers furnished a more complete body of information than had ever been recorded for the known tribes of the Lower Missouri and the Pacific Coast.

WESTERN DIPLOMACY

The Lewis and Clark expedition also had to be diplomatic. The Corps established an impressive record of peaceful contact with American Indians. In their limited way, Lewis and Clark honored the personal dignity of the American Indians.

Lewis and Clark had to notify every nation they met about the transfer of Louisiana Territory from France to the United States. As U.S. government representatives, the explorers offered aid, and tried to establish intertribal peace. "Follow these councils," Lewis said in his first speech, "and you will have nothing to fear because the great Spirit will smile upon your nation."[4] In spite of the clash of cultures, the Corps of Discovery made more friends than enemies.

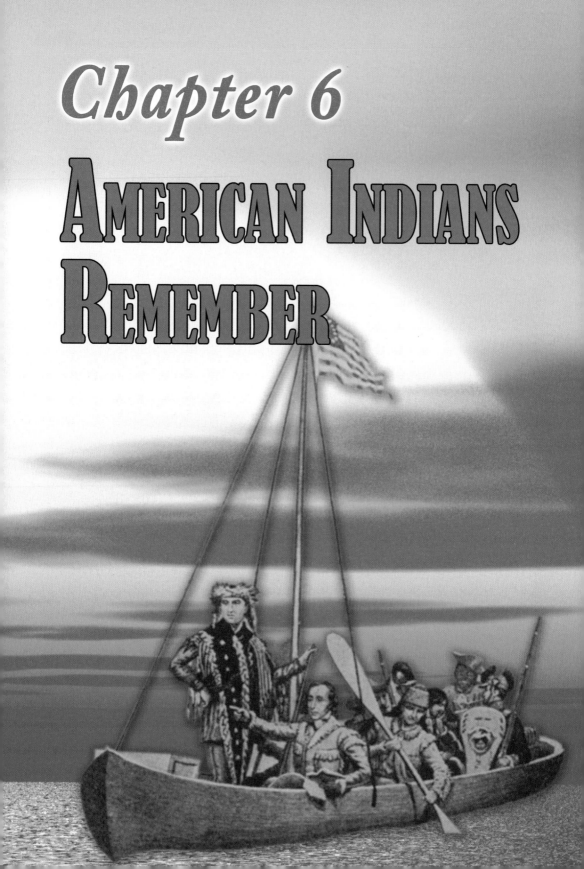

Chapter 6
American Indians Remember

Thomas Jefferson

knew the Louisiana Territory was a busy world populated by Indian nations. He understood that their world changed because of contact with Europeans and Americans.[1] His goal for the Corps of Discovery was to gather information needed to create a system of trade in the Louisiana Territory. He wanted Lewis and Clark to make it clear that the American government was interested in fostering peace between tribes and in trading.[2]

Jefferson had many questions about the tribes who lived in the Louisiana Territory. He was also interested in assimilating American Indians and educating their youth in American schools. At one point, Jefferson wanted all Indians in the United States to live in the Louisiana Territory.[3]

THE IRONY OF "DISCOVERY"

Most Americans viewed the Corps of Discovery as heroes after the expedition. Some American Indians today are upset about this attitude. They feel the Corps did not discover much. American Indians already knew everything the Corps reported. There was a history of trade across the continent when Lewis and Clark arrived in the West. While the expedition became a legend in American eyes, it held less significance for American Indian nations. Many already had contact with European trappers, traders, and soldiers for as long as two centuries. The French had lived and intermarried with the Missouri River tribes for two or three generations. There were large numbers of racially mixed people living along the Mississippi and Missouri Rivers. Several of them joined the Corps of Discovery.

A Clash of Cultures

Many American Indians feel the Corps did not accurately describe their cultures or their encounters with Americans. The Salish recall the white friendship robes they gave Captains Lewis and Clark to sit on and to take on their journey. The Captains left them on the ground. The original dwellers of the Bitterroot Valley say the only things Americans did not take from them were these robes.[4]

Lewis and Clark did their best to follow President Jefferson's orders to have friendly relations with the Indian nations along the expedition route. But many descendants of American Indians feel the Corps had little respect for them. White men viewed Indians as uncivilized even though many had highly organized societies. Lewis and Clark did not always respond to Indian cultures in an open-minded way. Sometimes they stereotyped Indian people because of the actions of a few. There were times when American Indians stole items from the Corps. Sometimes the thefts happened because someone was not paid fairly. Other thefts were criminal in nature.

Lewis and Clark tended to see all Indians as scheming rascals when thefts were committed. Lewis became angry at Indian thefts and killed people for stealing possessions. Lewis and a member of his party killed two Blackfeet men on the return journey over thefts of weapons and horses. Yet the Corps also stole horses, firewood, and a canoe from the Indians. They felt their thefts were necessary to the expedition's success.[5]

Lewis and Clark wrote ethnographic studies of the American Indians. But their methods of gathering information were not up to modern standards and they ignored many things. They judged everything they saw based on reason and logic, the philosophy of the Enlightenment. They called Indian ways "savage" when they did not understand them. The spiritual mysteries the Indians shared sounded like superstitions. The Corps ignored these stories and called them extraordinary. Many Indians found Christian mysteries equally extraordinary.

The explorers became close to the Mandan while they wintered near Mitutanka, a village of earth lodges. The Mandan had enjoyed commerce with Europeans for many decades. Their villages were a market exchange center for Indian and European goods.[6] Private Whitehouse wrote in April 1805 about the Mandan, "They are in general peaceable and well-disposed people."[7]

Lewis and Clark were careful about describing tribes that had little contact with white men. They found much to admire about Sacagawea's people, the Shoshone. Lewis called them "frank, communicative, fair in dealing, generous with the little they possess, extreemly honest, and by no means beggarly."[8] And they described the Walla Walla as "the most hospitable, honest, sincere people that we have met with in our voyage."[9]

FIFTY NATIONS

Nearly fifty American Indian nations met or had some contact with the Corps of Discovery. Some tribes were not impressed with the Corps. They did not even record their visit with them. None of the Plains Indians' "winter counts" from 1804 to 1805 had pictures representing the expedition. The "winter counts" were pictograph calendars painted on animal hides. Other events that winter were much more important to these people. According to oral histories, American Indians were

The Mandan became close to the members of the Corps of Discovery. Unfortunately, as Americans began emigrating west, American Indians lost their way of life. This George Catlin painting from 1832 shows Mandan Indian Mah-to-toh-pah, or Four Bears.

The Jefferson peace medals did not always win over the Indians. Lakota artist Paha Ska, an Elder of the Oglala Sioux tribe from the Pine Ridge Indian Reservation in South Dakota, holds an authentic Jefferson peace medal on December 17, 2001. Lewis and Clark gave this medallion to Indian leaders in 1803.

most fascinated by York, Captain Clark's slave. They also enjoyed Captain Lewis's Newfoundland dog. They admired steel knives and axes, magnifying glasses, mirrors, and the mysteries of the compass and sextant.[10] They either feared or enjoyed Lewis's loud air gun. It shot multiple balls without reloading, unlike the standard rifles of the day.

Lewis and Clark worried about carrying enough trade goods on the expedition. Some nations used to trading with white visitors were puzzled and offended by the Corps' stinginess. Some scoffed at the peace medals with Jefferson's likeness and the honorary certificates from the U.S. government. The Hidatsa felt the expedition's trinkets were tainted with evil. They passed them on to their enemies. One Cheyenne chief gave his medal back to Clark.[11]

Many tribes were disgusted with Lewis and Clark's bad manners and haughtiness. During their councils, the Captains spoke to the Indians in patronizing ways, calling them children and portraying Jefferson as their great father. Lewis and Clark did not understand that American Indians believed they were children of the Earth, governed by a higher power.

MORE ALIKE THAN DIFFERENT

Some of the claims made by white historians about historic "firsts" appear arrogant to modern Indian nations. Modern Indians are amused by historic claims that the Corps of Discovery held the first democratic elections west of the Mississippi when members voted about which fork of the Missouri to follow or which side of the Columbia River to camp on.[12] In fact, the U.S.

government modeled itself not only on Greek democracy, but also on the American Indian confederations in the East.

American Indian nations had organized societies similar to American communities of the same size. Their settlements sometimes had even more people than white settlements in the East. The combined Mandan villages had a population larger than St. Louis or Washington, D.C.

"If We Eat, You Shall Eat"

American Indians made it possible for the Corps of Discovery to complete its journey. Without their kind help, it is doubtful the Corps could have traveled from the United States to the Pacific coast and back with only one casualty. American Indians donated and traded food when the Corps ran out of supplies and when game was scarce. They had superior knowledge of the plants and animals "discovered" by Lewis and Clark. Indians offered directions, guides, and horses to the Corps. The Corps even adopted the American Indian-style clothing made of deer, buffalo, and elk skins when their uniforms and boots decayed.

Memories of Lewis and Clark

American Indians who had contact with the Corps of Discovery have passed down many stories about Lewis and Clark. These stories were told orally through many generations. Not until the late nineteenth and early twentieth century were these stories recorded in writing.

The Corps did not record as much as they could have about Arikara culture. They noted features valued by white culture: secure lodges, orderly fields, and well-tended crops. But the expedition left a strong impression on the Arikara. They were used to whites, but had never seen such a large party before. The Arikara were impressed by the Corps' technology. Above all things, they liked Clark's slave, York. They found special power—"medicine"—in his color and size. He played with their children, pretending to be a wild bear.

Captains Lewis and Clark enjoyed their warm friendship with the Nez Perce. Descendants of Red Bear, who talked with Clark, recall their ancestors sharing dogs with the Corps even though they never ate dogs themselves.[13] Even though the Nez Perce helped the Corps and were friendly to the U.S. government, the United States later forced the Nez Perce to leave their beloved land.

In October 1805, Yellept of the Walla Walla asked the Corps to stay longer so more of his people could see the visitors. He invited the explorers to come back. On the return trip, relations between the two groups grew even warmer. A Shoshone woman whom the Walla Walla had captured translated Walla Walla to Shoshone

The Shoshone were very important in helping Lewis and Clark survive their journey. Northern Shoshone tribal member Randy'l Hedow Teton is dressed in traditional Shoshone clothing and pictured with a horse wearing a traditional Indian saddle.

for Sacagawea. She then started the translation chain for Lewis and Clark.

The Clatsop were also friendly and supportive to the Corps. The Clatsop and their relatives, the Chinook, owned European clothing and many types of European trade goods. They had traded with Europeans for decades. Many sprinkled their speech with English words. The modern relatives of the Clatsop chief Coboway know what Lewis wrote in his journal about him: "He was much more kind [and] hospitable to us than any other indian in this neighbourhood."[14]

OPENING THE WEST

The Louisiana Purchase and the Corps of Discovery's expedition opened the West to a rush of settlers hungry for more land and resources. Americans and Indians were already engaged in a clash of cultures following white settlement from the Atlantic coast to the Ohio River. Many whites did not understand or agree with Indian ideas about land use. Settlers seized Indian lands and pushed tribes westward.[15]

The Corps of Discovery promised the American Indian nations trade and protection. But settlers, miners, and traders feared American Indian military power and stole their land. The United States government forced survivors to assimilate into American society. Epidemics of smallpox and other deadly diseases had already wiped out villages and tribes on both sides of the Mississippi before the expedition. Within a few short years, more disease, unfair treaties, wars, and forced marches to reservations reduced American Indian populations again. Many American Indian nations are still working to heal themselves and their cultures.

Chapter 7

A Sense of Pride

The thirty-three permanent members of the Corps of Discovery went in many different directions after their voyage. Very little is known about some of them, and many died young.[1]

Before returning to civilization in 1806, William Clark offered to care for Jean Baptiste Charbonneau. He supported the boy, who lived at a Catholic boarding school. At eighteen, Baptiste traveled to Europe. When he returned from Europe six years later, he headed west and worked as a trapper for many years. In 1866, Baptiste headed for a gold rush in Montana, but died of pneumonia at sixty-one after crossing a frigid river on horseback. He outlived all the members of the Corps, except Patrick Gass. Gass died at age ninety-eight in West Virginia on April 2, 1870.

The Fate of Clark and Corps Members

In March 1807, President Jefferson appointed Meriwether Lewis as governor of the Louisiana Territory. He appointed William Clark as chief Indian agent and brigadier general of the militia. They worked together in St. Louis, maintaining the friendship they shared on the expedition.

Clark married Julia Hancock immediately after the expedition. He was successful in business and widely respected. Explorers, traders, and mountain men visited him on their way through St. Louis. He continued to incorporate their findings into his detailed map of the West. American Indians considered Clark a friend and called him "the red-headed chief."[2]

In May 1807, Nathaniel Pryor's party, which included George Shannon, George Gibson, and possibly the Field brothers, departed from St. Louis with Mandan chief Sheheke. They attempted to return the chief and his family home to the Mandan villages in today's North Dakota. But they returned with Sheheke after an attack by the Arikara in October 1807.

Joseph Field died sometime between June 27 and October 20, 1807, the first veteran to die after the expedition. York went with Clark to St. Louis, who separated him from his wife in Louisville, Kentucky. Several of Clark's slaves were not happy with the move. York asked for his freedom or to be allowed to work in Louisville. A rift grew between them. Two years later Clark granted York's wish and hired him out in Louisville. About ten years after the expedition, Clark finally granted York his freedom. York went into the freighting business in Tennessee and Kentucky. York died of cholera around 1832.[3] William Clark died at the home of his oldest son, Meriwether Lewis Clark, on September 1, 1838.

THE TRAGIC DEATH OF MERIWETHER LEWIS

The most disturbing death of all the Corps of Discovery veterans was that of Meriwether Lewis. He had been suited to military and frontier life. But his new job as governor wore him down.

Lewis began to have difficulty handling the demands of political life in St. Louis. A young woman he was interested in married someone else. And though the expedition had been inspiring, he may have started to see it as a failure. No U.S. trading empire was established or seemed possible. American Indians remained in control of the Missouri River and were at war with one another. Worse, the expedition journals had not been published.

During the winter and spring of 1809, Lewis planned and packed for the company expedition. But he started drinking heavily. His journals show he took medicine for malaria that contained opium. His behavior became erratic.

What seemed to put Lewis over the edge was a letter from U.S. Secretary of War William Eustis.

He was already in debt. The War Department said it would not honor a large draft he had written for Indian gifts. Thomas Jefferson was impatient about the delay of the Corps journal publication. Lewis said he would go to Washington and Philadelphia to sort out his debts and again try to publish the journals.

Lewis started his journey three weeks later. As his boat traveled down the Mississippi River in September 1809, the crew said he tried to kill himself twice. On September 11, he wrote a will leaving all his possessions to his mother. Finally, on the sixth or seventh day of the journey, Lewis's mental health improved.

Lewis had planned to sail from New Orleans to Washington. But the party would instead travel by horseback on the heavily traveled Natchez Trace. British ships were prowling the Atlantic, and Lewis worried that the journals might fall into their hands.

It took the party three days to travel one hundred miles. Lewis began to drink, and his behavior became erratic again. After resting for two days, Lewis rode ahead of the party and promised to wait at the first house belonging to a white man. Late in the afternoon, Lewis arrived at Grinder's Inn, a log cabin where overnight visitors stayed. During the early hours of October 11, he shot himself in the head and chest. The suicide hurt Lewis's

Lewis posed for this painting in 1807. Just two years later, he committed suicide.

reputation in his day. It would be one hundred years before Thwaites' edition of the journals restored the good names of Lewis and Clark.

SACAGAWEA STORIES

Historians have many different views about the life of Sacagawea. She was said to be a Shoshone, who was captured and enslaved by the Hidatsa.

99

There is evidence to prove she died at the age of twenty-five at Fort Manuel on December 20, 1812. But many American Indians disagree. They think Americans mixed up Charbonneau's second wife with Sacagawea.

Today's Hidatsa say Sacagawea was one of them. A Hidatsa named Bullseye told a convincing story about Sacagawea to a Major Welch in 1925. He claims she had more children and was his grandmother. He said the Hidatsa did not capture her. He claims she walked along the Missouri River to her home near the Knife River after traveling west with her father. They made the journey just one year before the Corps of Discovery came to the Mandan villages. He explained that Cameahwait's relationship as "brother" to Sacagawea was an American Indian term. It meant he was a friend of the same age, or a cousin. Because she did not speak French or English, Bullseye believed that interpreters mixed up her story. He said she died at age eighty-two in 1869 when the Assiniboin or Yanktonai attacked her family in present-day Montana.[4]

LEARNING FROM LEWIS AND CLARK

Historian James Ronda wrote that the voyage of the Corps of Discovery was not a "tour of discovery through an empty West," but a "diverse human

Sacagawea may have died at age twenty-five at Fort Manuel on December 20, 1812. This statue of her was erected on May 24, 2003, in Salmon, Idaho. It is rumored to be near her burial site.

community moving through the lands and lives of other communities."[5] Today, historians are still learning more details about the Lewis and Clark expedition. Although the journey ended more than two hundred years ago, its legacy still lives in American history.

Chapter Notes

Chapter 1. Creature Feature

1. Gary E. Moulton, ed., *The Definitive Journals of Lewis and Clark* (Lincoln, Nebr.: University of Nebraska Press, 1987), vol. 4, pp. 289–291.

2. Paul Schullery, *Lewis and Clark Among the Grizzlies* (Guilford, Conn. and Helena, Mont.: Globe Pequot Press, 2002), pp. 34, 85–89.

3. Ibid.

4. Moulton, p. 294.

5. Stephen E. Ambrose, *Undaunted Courage: Meriwether Lewis, Thomas Jefferson, and the Opening of the American West* (New York: Ambrose-Tubbs, Inc., 1996), pp. 238–239.

Chapter 2. Westward View

1. Stephen E. Ambrose, *Undaunted Courage: Meriwether Lewis, Thomas Jefferson, and the Opening of the American West* (New York: Ambrose-Tubbs, Inc., 1996), p. 20.

2. Ibid., p. 26.

3. Ibid., p. 24.

4. Ibid., p. 32.

5. Ibid., pp. 46–50.

6. William E. Foley, *Wilderness Journey: The Life of William Clark* (Columbia, Miss.: University of Missouri Press, 2004), pp. 4–5.

7. Ibid.

8. Ibid., p. 15

9. James J. Holmberg, *Dear Brother: Letters of William Clark to Jonathan Clark* (New Haven & London: Yale University Press, 2002), p. 57.

10. Ambrose, p. 98.

11. Foley, p. 51.

Chapter 3. An Epic Journey

1. David W. Hogan, Jr., and Charles E. White, eds., *The U.S. Army and the Lewis and Clark Expedition* (Washington, D.C.: Center of Military History Publication 70-71-1), p. 7.

2. "Lewis and Clark Voyage of Rediscovery," 2002, <http://www.voyageofrediscovery.com/part2/historical/index.shtml> (November 30, 2008).

3. Hogan and White, pp. 6–8.

4. Ibid.

5. "Lewis and Clark: Journey of Discovery," National Park Service, n.d.,<http://www.nps.gov/archive/jeff/zlewisclark2/CorpsOfDiscovery/Preparing/Preparing.htm> (November 30, 2008).

6. "Lewis and Clark: Historical Background," National Park Service, February 22, 2004, <http://www.nps.gov/history/history/online_books/lewisandclark/intro1.htm> (November 30, 2008).

7. Dayton Duncan and Ken Burns, *Lewis and Clark: Journey of the Corps of Discovery* (New York: Alfred A. Knopf, 1997), p. 22.

8. Stephen E. Ambrose, *Undaunted Courage: Meriwether Lewis, Thomas Jefferson, and the Opening of the American West* (New York: Ambrose-Tubbs, Inc., 1996), pp. 100–132.

9. Gary E. Moulton, ed., *The Lewis and Clark Journals: An American Epic of Discovery*, Abridgement of the Definitive Nebraska Edition (Lincoln, Nebr.: University of Nebraska Press, 2003), p. 1.

10. Bruce C. Paton, *Lewis and Clark: Doctors in the Wilderness* (Golden, Colo.: Fulcrum Publishing, 2001), pp. 88–90.

11. Ambrose, p. 156.

12. James P. Ronda, *Lewis and Clark Among the Indians* (Lincoln, Nebr.: University of Nebraska Press, 1998), p. 30.

13. Ronda, pp. 28–40.

14. Ambrose, p. 211.

15. Ibid., pp. 248–249.

16. Moulton, Abridgement, p. 205.

17. Gary E. Moulton, ed., *The Definitive Journals of Lewis & Clark: Down the Columbia to Fort Clatsop* (Lincoln, Nebr.: University of Nebraska Press, 2002), vol. 6, p. 33.

18. Ambrose, p. 313.

19. Moulton, *The Definitive Journals*, pp. 138–189.

20. Ibid., p. 171.

21. Ambrose, pp. 335–336.

Chapter 4. Heading Home

1. Gary E. Moulton, ed., *The Definitive Journals of Lewis & Clark: From the Pacific to the Rockies* (Lincoln, Nebr.: University of Nebraska Press, 2002), vol. 7, p. 52.

2. Stephen E. Ambrose, *Undaunted Courage: Meriwether Lewis, Thomas Jefferson, and the Opening of the American West* (New York: Ambrose-Tubbs, Inc., 1996), p. 393.

3. Moulton, vol. 8, p. 136.

4. Ibid., p. 138.

5. Ibid., p. 158.

Chapter 5. A Failed Mission?

1. Stephen E. Ambrose, *Undaunted Courage: Meriwether Lewis, Thomas Jefferson, and the Opening of the American West* (New York: Ambrose-Tubbs, Inc., 1996), p. 94.

2. "To the Western Ocean: Planning the Lewis and Clark Expedition: Overview, May 24," *Lewis and Clark: The Maps of Exploration 1507–1814*, 2007,

<http://www.lib.virginia.edu/small/exhibits/lewis_clark/planning.html> (November 30, 2008).

3. Dayton Duncan and Ken Burns, *Lewis and Clark: Journey of the Corps of Discovery* (New York: Alfred A. Knopf, 1997), pp. 36–37.

4. Ibid., p. 233

Chapter 6. American Indians Remember

1. Stephen E. Ambrose, *Undaunted Courage: Meriwether Lewis, Thomas Jefferson, and the Opening of the American West* (New York: Ambrose-Tubbs, Inc., 1996), p. 78.

2. James P. Ronda, *Lewis and Clark Among the Indians* (Lincoln, Nebr.: University of Nebraska Press, 1998), pp. 4–5.

3. Ambrose, pp. 55–57.

4. Alvin M. Josephy, Jr., *Lewis and Clark through Indian Eyes* (New York: Alfred A. Knopf, 2006), p. 40.

5. Thomas Slaughter, *Exploring Lewis and Clark: Reflections on Men and Wilderness* (New York: Alfred A. Knopf, 2003), p. 161.

6. Ronda, p. 67.

7. Gary E. Moulton, ed., *The Definitive Journals of Lewis & Clark: The Journals of Joseph Whitehouse, May 14, 1804–April 2, 1806* (Lincoln, Nebr.: University of Nebraska Press, 2002), vol. 11, p. 132.

8. Gary E. Moulton, ed., *The Lewis and Clark Journals: An American Epic of Discovery,* Abridgement of the Definitive Nebraska Edition (Lincoln, Nebr.: University of Nebraska Press, 2003), pp. 93, 189.

9. Moulton, *The Definitive Journals*, vol. 7. pp. 196–197.

10. Ronda, p. 23.

11. Josephy, pp. 152–153.

12. Slaughter, pp. 16–17.

13. Ibid, pp. 40–43.

14. James P. Ronda, *Finding the West: Explorations with Lewis and Clark* (Albuquerque, N.M.: University of New Mexico Press, 2001), p. 127.

15. Ronda, *Lewis and Clark Among the Indians*, pp. 254–255.

Chapter 7. A Sense of Pride

1. Dayton Duncan and Ken Burns, *Lewis and Clark: Journey of the Corps of Discovery* (New York: Alfred A. Knopf, 1997), p. 211.

2. Ibid., pp. 221–222.

3. Larry E. Morris, *The Fate of the Corps* (New Haven and London: Yale University Press, 2004), pp. 29–30.

4. William E. Foley, *Wilderness Journey: The Life of William Clark* (Columbia, Mo.: University of Missouri Press, 2004), pp. xi, 236.

5. Alvin M. Josephy, Jr., *Lewis and Clark through Indian Eyes* (New York: Alfred A. Knopf, 2006), pp. 129–134.

Glossary

anatomy—The structure of an animal or plant.

anthropologist—A scientist who studies the physical, social, and cultural development of humans.

assimilate—To conform to the customs and attitudes of a group or nation.

botanical—Referring to plants or plant life and the science of botany.

cache—A hidden storage space; to save up for future use.

cartographer—A person who makes maps.

casualty—A member of the armed forces lost to service through death, wounds, sickness, or capture.

confluence—Junction of two rivers.

council—An assembly or meeting for consultation, advice, or discussion.

diplomacy—Tact and skill in dealing with people and in negotiating agreements, alliances, and treaties.

draftsman—A person who draws plans and sketches of buildings, maps, or machines.

Enlightenment—An eighteenth-century philosophical movement focused on the power of reason.

espontoon—A six-foot-long half-pike or spear carried by eighteenth-century infantry officers.

ethnography—The branch of anthropology that deals with the scientific description of specific human cultures.

ethnology—The science that analyzes and compares human cultures.

interpreter—A person who provides translation between people who speak different languages.

Louisiana Purchase—The 1803 treaty between France and the United States in which the U.S. purchased land extending from the Mississippi River to the Rocky Mountains and from Canada to the Gulf of Mexico.

morale—Confidence in the face of hardship.

portage—Carrying boats overland from one water source to another.

quell—To overwhelm, quiet, reduce, or stop.

reservation—A tract of public land set aside for use by American Indians.

sextant—A navigational instrument used to measure the altitudes of the sun, moon, and stars to determine latitude and longitude.

stereotype—To describe a person with an overly simple image or type.

terrain—The physical features of a tract of land.

voyage—An act or instance of traveling; journey.

voyageur—An expert woodsman, boatman, and guide in remote regions. Voyageurs were employed by eighteenth- and nineteenth-century fur companies to transport supplies to and from their distant stations. Also called engagés.

Further Reading

BOOKS

Blumberg, Rhoda. *York's Adventures with Lewis and Clark: An African-American's Part in the Great Expedition*. New York: HarperCollins Publishers, 2004.

Burrows, John. *Lewis & Clark: Blazing a Trail West*. New York: Sterling, 2008.

Crosby, Michael T. *Sacagawea: Lewis and Clark's Pathfinder*. Stockton, N.J.: OTTN Pub., 2008.

Johmann, Carol A. *The Lewis & Clark Expedition: Join the Corps of Discovery to Explore Uncharted Territory*. Charlotte, Vt.: Williamson Pub., 2003.

Patent, Dorothy Hinshaw. *Animals on the Trail with Lewis and Clark*. New York: Clarion Books, 2002.

———. *Plants on the Trail with Lewis and Clark*. New York: Clarion Books, 2003.

Rodger, Ellen. *Lewis and Clark: Opening the American West*. New York: Crabtree, 2005.

INTERNET ADDRESSES

Discovering Lewis & Clark

<http://www.lewis-clark.org/>

The Journals of the Lewis and Clark Expedition

<http://lewisandclarkjournals.unl.edu/index.html>

Lewis and Clark Trail Heritage Foundation

<http://www.lewisandclark.org/>

Index